Cash - N - Checks

A relationship guide to money

Richard Mullen

ISBN: 9798625843690
Imprint: Independently published

Editor: Erin Olenjack

Library of Congress Control Number: 2020905129
Printed in the United States of America

I dedicate this book to my 20-something niece Staci, who once said, "Wow Uncle Rich, you sure know a lot about this. You should write a book. I'd buy it."

TABLE OF CONTENTS:

Forward:

For the first half of my life I lived in the nightmare of the American relationship with money. My parents, in the 1970's, were chronic under-wage earners. My father was in law enforcement and my mother flitted between jobs, preferring to be a homemaker over working outside the home. In a time when cops were paid only slightly more than teachers, who made little more than the military -who were mostly on food stamps and living in substandard housing on base- this caused a lot of strife in our house.

It was also a time when the Man-of-the-House wasn't questioned in his decisions and did not share any of the details with his children, because it wasn't their business. This approach is detrimental to the financial success of the next generation. After all, we teach how to shake hands and look someone in the eye, so why don't we teach financial savvy?

We moved to Tacoma, Washington, in 1979 and it didn't get any better. Eventually their marriage crumbled as they grew apart and, like many families where one was the sole support of the other, my mother tried to rely upon my father for financial support through the divorce decree. For obvious reasons this was nearly impossible and resulted in my father supporting two households on one income. Being in high school at the time -a time when America was coming into its prime, at the top of the Cold War 1980's cocaine fueled rush, New Wave Music, and international everything- set me back by trying to live in the middle class when my family income was really lower class. No blame here, this is just the truth.

A guide to chasing the American dream of the day:

Step 1.) Go to College. Doesn't matter where. Doesn't matter why. Pay for it with student loans.

Step 2.) Get a good job with a 401k and a big paycheck. Doesn't matter where, why, or how. No one knew that 1991 would be a recession and it was all about who you knew, not necessarily what you were educated in (unless it was hard science, law, or the medical field).

Step 3.) Acquire the accoutrements of success. Wife, cars, kids, house, etc. Pay for it with credit, pay the minimum balance, and live in debt.

Step 4.) Retire to somewhere nice. Bounce grandkids on knee. Travel the world.

But as the Little Prince said, *"A goal without a plan is a wish."*

This book is the result of my growing up, getting kicked in the teeth, learning how to adult, eventually becoming a financial mentor, and hoping to God that *someone* younger than me will listen to my lessons and avoid the mistakes I have made. That someday, they will navigate their own ship into their own port and have the life that they will have earned.

Introduction:

There are dozens of books on money management, how to accumulate wealth, change your relationship with wealth, etc. The difference between them and this book is that I will tell you what to do right here.

You need to become the Master of your Money.

And how do you do that? Live on less than you earn, avoid debt, and invest in something that will earn more interest than inflation.

This is easier said than done.

The following chapters will cover the essential idea that changing our relationship with money is really rooted in how we perceive ourselves as users of money. Why do we spend the way we do? What are our defined goals? Why are we working?

Once you can answer these questions for yourself, then you can change your approach to money, both using and earning. Here is an essential idea, your goals, the reason why you are working and the things that you want, are only important to you and once you can recognize what is important, and why, you can then make targeted decisions to provide yourself with them. Therefore, if an expensive car is vitally important to you, no one else's opinion is important. The question that remains is simple. How are you going to pay for it without selling your soul?

Living on less than you earn

Chapter 1

I know that everyone has heard this before, "work hard, save your money." However, how much money and how to save it are the lingering questions. It takes approximately 90% of pre-retirement income to maintain your lifestyle in retirement. It follows that if you save 10% of your income, it will take you 100 years to save enough money to retire for 10 years. If you start working at 18 years old, you will have to work until you are 118 to be able to retire until you are 128. Then you must die because you're out of money. If you have the secret to live to be 100, please publish it so you can make enough money to retire early, then I can buy your book and live to be 100 too.

Assuming you are living hand to mouth, paycheck to paycheck, it is almost impossible to conceive that you can live on less than you earn. We will get to that next. If you don't, then all your money is going to someone else. You are a de facto slave. The fruit of your labor, your money, isn't your money. It belongs to Visa, MasterCard, the car company, Starbucks, the cell phone company, and the landlord. You get my point. The first person who has to get paid is you.

Understand that if you max out your credit cards, have a car loan, have a cell phone bill that includes a loan for the phone, or maybe have a mortgage, you are beholden to someone else. Once you free yourself from these bills, you free yourself to pursue your true goals in life. Most people are living in debt, paycheck to paycheck, working towards death. Living only to provide an income for someone else. Living to work. Living in slavery.

Every month the bills come due. I am not talking about the fixed expenses like housing, although these are recurring. I am talking about the expenses that can and do change on a monthly basis. Christmas and time to give big gifts! It's New Year's Eve, St Patrick's Day, Cinco de Mayo, whatever, got to throw the big party! Summer is here and time to go on the most epic adventure! Maybe it's Friday and time to cut loose from the work week. Whatever your expense, and don't tell me you rarely do any of this because the current national consumer debt suggests otherwise, these bills come due and paying the minimum on the credit card won't make them go away. If anything, the debt just compounds, and it all gets more expensive. Trust me on this, the bank may pay you interest quarterly, but they will charge you interest daily. That is the difference in your interest rate on your credit card and the loan. Your credit card interest is their profit. The interest on your account is your profit. Go figure, you are going to make less than the bank does, that's another way the bank makes money off of *You*. Remember that the credit card rate says X%, however, your annual percentage rate (APR) is slightly higher. That's so you can do the dumb math and quick calculate the interest on your purchase over one year. Pro tip for you, the credit card companies don't want you to pay off your cards. EVER. If you buy something on credit and you make only the minimum payments, you will pay whatever the APR is as part of the purchase price. So, if it is a pair of jeans for $100 and your credit card APR is the national average of 19.02%, and you take 1 year to pay for those jeans, you just paid $119, or essentially 20% more, than they were originally priced.

Most people believe a budget is where you take the money you earn, portion it out to pay your bills, and what is left over you use for saving or investing or fun money or whatever. Budgets are for CHUMPS! A budget is what you do when you don't control your money. A way for you to think of yourself as money conscious and in control. In reality, you are trying to juggle your funds to cover your mistakes.

A typical budget may look something like this:

<u>BUDGET</u>

RENT/MORTGAGE	$1,500
GROCERIES (food in home only)	$393
CAR PAYMENT	$550
CAR INSURANCE	$135
CELL PHONE (per line)	$70
UTILITIES	$253

INTERNET	$100
DINING OUT (Per person)	$242

==

TOTAL	$3,243.00
INCOME (after taxes)	$4,362.00
Available for savings	$1,740.00

I know you're having an immediate reaction to this, that there is something wrong with my numbers. These numbers above were taken from a simple internet search using the search phrase "average XXX per month in the US." Average gross pay in the US is $64,154.00 and take home is $52,344.00. The factoring continues below, we're just getting started.

There is also a disconnect here. First, individual tax rates are different. The above is a mixed bag of numbers including household averages and individual averages. Because some expenses like household expenses exist regardless of the number of people in the household. I have also used the terms median and average interchangeably but this is inaccurate as the average isn't the median, but usually higher than the median, which is the number in the middle of two different numbers- i.e. the median between 1 and 1,000,000 is 500,000 but the average of them is 500,000.5. A slight but mathematical difference.

This example shows that the individual here has a potential for saving $1,740/month, which is 39.88%. However, is it actually 32.5%. Remember the above $52k is after taxes. But wait! It is said that most people aren't making it. What did I forget?

CHILDCARE (OFTEN PER CHILD)	$972
DINNERS (+ WHOLE FAMILY)	$726
ALCOHOL (YEAH RIGHT)	$50
COFFEE/SODA/SNACKS	$100
GASOLINE	$250
HEALTH INSURANCE (INDIVIDUAL)	$441
(FAMILY)	$1,168

==

TOTAL (WITHOUT INSURANCE)	$2,098.00
SAVINGS ($1,740.00 - $2,098)	-$358.00
Plus, INSURANCE (INDIVIDUAL)	-$799.00
(FAMILY)	-$1,526.00

This doesn't include Netflix, Hulu or iTunes, Amazon prime, or any of the unconscious spending that we do every day.

I hear a question from the back of the room, "What is unconscious spending?" Unconscious spending is the gadgets at the register that you can't live without. The candy bars. The tabloid magazines. Oooh! A bright pink thingy. It is the soda when you stop for gas, the candy bar, or quick bag of chips on the long road trip. Unconscious spending is usually less than $10, more often $5 or less, and that you think "hey, it's only a couple of bucks." It comes from the same logic as the $XX.99 pricing. It's $14.99 isn't that only $14? No, it's $15, your brain is just tricking you into thinking it's only $14. On average, in my experience as a financial mentor, I have seen that most people spend $200 average, per month in unconscious spending. I once counseled someone who was spending over $700 per month in unconscious spending.

You can find your unconscious spending with a highlighter and your monthly credit or debit card statement. Scan through the statement and any purchase that you cannot identify immediately highlight it. Like I said previously, it's probably less than $10, and you can't remember what it was. Often these expenditures are close to other costs like gas. You can also find the unconscious spending on your receipts from the grocery store. Individual items like a 20oz soda, or a candy bar, are much cheaper if you buy them in bigger packages like the 12 pack of soda. Do you really need a soda for the ride home? This is the behavior I am here to address. The relationship we have with the use of money.

In the awesome, *Your Money or Your Life*, the authors' attempt to make you understand how much life a cup of coffee costs. This is how I break it down:

On average the life expectancy in the US is 78.69 years. Let's round up to 80 for simplicity's sake. Your first 20 years, you are a child and your life isn't yours to provide for yourself so subtract 20 and now we have 60 years left. You will spend 1/3 of your remaining 60 years, (assuming 8 hours per day) in bed, asleep. Now you have 40 years left. You will spend 1/3 of the original 60 at work. Work here includes anything that isn't necessarily fun. Mowing the grass, doing laundry, washing the car, or actually at a job. Now you have 20 years left. You will spend approximately 122 days of your life waiting for red lights, alone. If you add waiting in lines, you spend almost FIVE YEARS OF YOUR LIFE waiting in line. Now you have 15 years left. If you have been keeping track that makes you 65 years old. Remember that the average life expectancy is actually 78.69 years. In reality, you only have 13 years left. There are other things that take away from our life clock, like genetics and lifestyle and God's sick sense of humor.

At the time of writing this, the US federal minimum wage is $7.25 per hour. If a Grande latte is $3.65 and a blueberry scone is $2.45, you just spent $6.10 on breakfast. Now calculate the minimum wage as a representative of the time you have to live; that latte and scone equal 50.4 minutes of *Your LIFE*. So how much is that cup of coffee and a muffin worth? This doesn't even include the time you spent waiting in line for it. Taking that into account, let's just round it up to the hour. Remember that pair of jeans? $120 is the equivalent of 16.6 hours of your life, or basically one day awake. I hope those jeans make you look good.

My thanks to the authors of *Your Money or your Life* because if I had never read your book, I would never have learned this. At least not early on in my life. What do you need to do to improve your relationship with money? Examine how you are spending your money, and why you are spending your money this way.

In my house, we spend every Saturday and Sunday morning making a big breakfast. Eggs, hash browns (from scratch), bacon or sausage or steak or pork chops, toast, coffee, and juice (usually from scratch). There isn't a diner on earth that can tempt us. A national chain offers this same breakfast for $14.47 per person (or two hours of your life). If we go cheap and just do bacon, then we're usually under $4.00 for 4 people and we shared the time together to make it. Sometimes we splurge and lay out the whole Mediterranean flair with goat cheese bruschetta, some other dried cheeses like Manchego and Asiago or Parmesan, some sliced deli meats, olives, and pickles, and smoked salmon, a loaf of bread or bagels toasted, and some fruit. In the end we might spend $15 on the whole thing. Again, for 4 people. We do this same idea with baked goods like muffins, or cookies. Tacos on Tuesday, every Tuesday, and homemade pizza on Fridays. Pi day (March 14, the day when all food must be consumed in the form of a pie) is a serious affair in my house with homemade quiche, empanadas, pot pies and dessert pie.

Anyone can do this. Can't cook? You can YouTube it. Don't have time? Don't tell me you don't have time. This is part of the change you need to make in your relationship with money. Learning how to cook is learning how to save money. Learning how to save money takes time. The time you spend will save you money, which will give you more time later to not be working. You need to make this time a priority in your life. Put down the phone, until after you make dinner, then share *that* on social media. Life is busy. You can make every excuse in the book. I've heard them all and used half of them myself. Or, you can change your relationship with money. I did and now I no longer dread opening the emails from the bills. I just click paid.

I graduated college in 1991, approximately $40,000 in debt to student loans. In 2002, I joined the Navy, flat broke, and now $42,000 in debt. I had defaulted on my student loans (they don't go away by the way), had had most of my possessions repossessed (2 sailboats), and had accumulated a few thousand dollars in card debt. With my new income I managed to pay off some debt right away, but that damned student loan debt hung around my neck like a noose until January of 2010. In January 2010, I went on a cash only budget and by March of 2011 I paid off the entire $38k I still owed in student loans. During the whole process I paid close attention to the balance. With each payment made I could visibly see the principle drop. It would cause my heart to race when I would get the next bill and see how much the balance had dropped. Even though I knew that the last payment would cause a drop in the principle, it was a gut reaction to seeing the new balance reflect my efforts. To see the bill drop to $38,000. $37,000, eventually $29,000. And to see other bills I had at that time just disappear. Balance $0. It was a bigger thrill than the original purchase, a bigger thrill than receiving the college degree. In the moment of victory, I decided to celebrate. After all, what is life without some celebration? So, I saved up and took the family on the trip of a lifetime to Disneyland, where I paid cash for the whole trip.

We stayed right outside of the park and ate two out of three meals a day in the park. I didn't want for anything and not once was I concerned with the cost of anything. When I got home, I didn't have any bills left over to haunt me for having fun. Altogether, I paid off approximately $46,000 in debt and the trip. I will never forget the feeling, the day I received the zero-balance notice from my student loans. It was the last bill I had to pay off. It was Pi day and I was finally a free man.

The golden rule of saving is 10%, however, in the beginning this may be too much for you to start. But you have to set something aside for you. This is your life. Live it how you want to. That being said, unless you want to work for your entire life, and there are people who do, you need to start funding that life today. Remember that $16,000 invested at 18 years old, at 8% interest will yield $405,431.71 at 59 ½ years old. With no further investment after 42 years you would have approximately that amount of money if compounded annually. If compounded daily, the total would be closer to $500,000. Good luck finding a bank that will pay that kind of interest. You have to seek that level of return elsewhere and we will discuss that later.

Here is the equation for compounding interest-something Albert Einstein called the 8th wonder of the world;

Future Value $(FV) = \$16,000 \times (1 + (8\%/1)^{(1 \times 42)} = \$405,431.71$

The second main rule of saving is to KEEP YOUR DAMN HANDS OUT OF THE SAVINGS! If you don't, then your savings will never grow to anything worth anything. Like any garden, if you don't water it, fertilize it, and sometimes leave it alone, nothing will ever grow. You cannot expect your nest egg to ever develop into something worth crowing about if you keep making breakfast. Sometimes you have to dip into the well but, like Bob Marley said, "...every day the bucket go to the well, one day the bottom of it drop out."

Discipline is how you keep from picking at your savings. This discipline comes from the ultimate desire, the ultimate goal. What that goal is, is up to you and you alone. For me, the goal is a beach house where I can sit on the deck and look at my sailboat, and where I can sit on the deck of my sailboat and look at my beach house. In Zombieland, Tallahassee said to him the goal was "a Vortec… V-8, a box of hollow-points, and, the good Lord willing, a G-D Twinkie." Your goal is your goal. Once you pick this goal, come to an understanding of who you are and what this goal is for you. Then the determination to achieve this goal will be your discipline to let your savings grow. We will talk about that here shortly too.

How to live on less than you earn is a question many people have. First you need to examine how you are spending your money. Is a cell phone necessary? Is that specific car necessary? Did you need to go out to eat for lunch today? Where are those leftovers from going out yesterday? A lot of money is spent keeping up with the Kardashians. Let me tell you a secret, you can't. Keeping up with the Kardashians is a full-time job itself. You can't, you shouldn't try, and it's making you sad. Maybe killing you too.

Living on less than you earn is a matter of balancing your needs and your wants. Dr. Maslow established the hierarchy of needs. These needs are often confused. The pyramid begins with the physiological needs on the bottom and towards the top are the esteem needs. Most people think that the esteem needs are the true needs, the things they must have. But all that you really must have are food, clothing, and shelter. Next are safety needs. Resources like employment, health, and property. Next are love and belonging. Then esteem; the look at me stuff. You know, the iPhone, the Starbucks, the Cadillac, and all the likes on Facebook. Finally, at the top of the pyramid, is self-actualization or the desire to be the best you can be. Most people don't really look towards this until they are much older. The problem, and the thing that drives consumer society, is the confusion of esteem needs and physiological needs. The esteem needs make people feel good about themselves, which is why they are so easily confused with physiological needs. Beans and rice will keep you alive, but steak and ice cream will make you happy.

Here you need to decide how to balance your needs and wants. The dumb thing here is that if you don't know what you want, you cannot focus on meeting your needs or achieving your goals. If you cannot say, "I want a fancy car" you cannot say how you will shift your focus to achieve the fancy car.

Chapter 2

In full disclosure, it has been a minute since I lived at the poverty level but I did live there for many years. Minimum wage jobs, roach infested apartments, broke-ass rides that cost more money per mile than they were worth. Yeah, I lived there. How do you get out of this cycle? It isn't easy but what are you willing to do? In any tragedy, the ones who survive are the ones most willing to do whatever it takes to survive. This same idea is true to escape poverty. It's why sheetrock hangers and drug dealers become sheetrock hangers and drug dealers. No one ever grows up wanting to hang sheetrock or live the risky life of a drug dealer. Children grow up wanting to be something great, something with meaning and purpose. Those who find themselves in hard, or even dangerous jobs, do so because they are willing to do whatever it takes to make money.

The first way to break out of the poverty cycle is work. Being willing to take any job and pushing towards your goal relentlessly with the "immigrant mentality" is how you do this. Immigrant mentality is the mentality of accepting any job, working long hours, and saving every penny possible. Today we define this as hustle. Being willing to take a chance. Not being defined by what you do. This represents an overall drive and desire to succeed. If you want to change your relationship with money, you have got to change your mindset. I knew a man from the Philippines who came to work for me as a dishwasher in 1996. In the interview, he told me he would only come work for me for $13.65 per hour. At the time we were paying dishwashers approximately $6.00 per hour. I told him we couldn't support this and went and told the general manager, who asked me if I shook the man's hand. I said yes, it was like a chunk of 2X4, solid, calloused, firm. The GM said hire him, he makes $13.25 across the street. I hired the man, he dictated his schedule to me, and we never wanted for anything from him during his time in our employment. Minimum wage at the time was $5.14. He had made himself invaluable by his work ethic. He was one of the highest paid people in the store, and he always had an impressive roll of cash in his pocket. He had three jobs, two full time and one part-time. He drove a nicer car than I did. I was salaried at $30k per year with bonuses of 10% of the store's annual sales. The store did nearly $2 million annually.

Education is another way to escape the poverty level livelihood. The problem is if you're working long hours, the time to get an education is excessive to how many hours are in the day. If you don't have the money for your bills how can you get the money to go to school? What would you go to school to study? Do you go to school to get a degree in some random Bachelor's area and then hope to get a job in that area? How are you going to get a job in that area when you have no experience? Unless you go into the hard sciences, you need some form of experience otherwise your education is primarily theory only anyway. If you chose a trade school, you limit yourself to how much money you can earn in a year. If you become a mechanic, and we NEED mechanics, your maximum income is $40,710 annually, according to the national average. That is approximately $24k below the median income for the US.

So how do you determine what field to go into? The best resource available today has to be O*Net Online, https://www.onetonline.org/ . This website, established by the Department of Labor, has every job and career field available and the statistics and education requirements required by them. It's free, go online and check it out. You can research everything you need to know about any possible career field. It will even tell you if there is a future in your career field or if it is time to find another career. From the green industry to IT, if you want to pursue it, they have the information. How do you know what you might like to do for a career? There are several different tests you can take including the Meyers-Briggs, the military ASVAB test, and O*Net Online also has a quick test. You can even take an ASVAB online through militaryonsesource.com. This test can help you figure out what field you might be successful in, and from there check out O*net and find your future.

Shameless plug here, if you're between the ages of 17 - 34, go sit down with a military recruiter. They get paid to talk to people about careers and training. Just don't be offended if they tell you they cannot help you because you don't qualify. 80% of all Americans today cannot qualify to serve in the military, mostly for medical reasons. There are also recruiters in many different fields. If you're considering a job that has a union, go to the union hall and see what it takes to become trained in that field. Ask the questions. Seek out people in the field and ask them to sit down with you and talk about themselves. Most people love to.

Again, one of the most important tools to help you escape your situation is to figure out where you want to go. What is it you want? That beach house I spoke of, so far, it's a 3-bedroom, 2-bathroom, 1200 sq. foot bungalow. It ain't huge, won't ever be featured on an episode of MTV Cribs or on HGTV, but it will be mine and my mortgage will be less than half of what it could rent for. That is what I want. So how am I going to get it? By picking my own path, limiting my wants to my more pressing needs, and not buying into the fiscal nightmare of the American dream. I buy reconditioned cell phones, older models, still good enough but not expensive. I buy clothes at Goodwill (I own 7 pairs of Levi's, a Bottega Venetta Jacket, none of which I paid anything near full price for). I don't have to have anything. Well that's not entirely true. I do own a custom motorcycle. It's not a Harley, nor an Orange County Chopper, but it has custom paint, handlebars, seat, sissy bar etc. I paid cash for it and then added most of the additional parts by installing them myself. I saved thousands of dollars and still got what I wanted. No one is judging your wants. I am only trying to help you focus yourself to those wants that represent your vision of your successful self.

So, you're living at the poverty level. Perhaps you lack the education to get a better job. Perhaps you lack the opportunity to move somewhere else due to a lack of funds. You can change both of those. 76% of all Americans have internet access, and with that access you can learn almost anything. Reading a challenge? YouTube. Math a challenge? YouTube. No internet? The local library has all the books you could ever want to learn about anything and the internet too. Do not let your situation determine your destiny. That is up to you alone. Yes, you can change your destiny. It will not be easy but nothing worthwhile ever is. There are many civic programs out there to help. Yes, childcare can be an issue but perhaps you have a friend in a similar situation and together you can help each other. You can do it! You can! Truly! I believe in *You*! Even at poverty level living, the most important thing to do is pay yourself first. If you make minimum wage, you can save something every month. Just a few dollars at first. Find a bank account that has free savings and start with just $5 a week. It won't grow fast but it will grow.

Here is something that will seem almost contrary to what I am saying about savings. Spend a little on yourself too. If you are living at the poverty level, and you want to make a change in your life, give yourself a small stipend every week. This stipend is a small amount of money, less than $20, you can just blow on whatever you want. You don't need to account for it nor explain it to anyone. At the end of the week, if you didn't spend it you can either take out the same amount the following week or roll it over into savings.

Eventually you will find that you don't need to spend it but, if you do, it doesn't matter anyway. This relief valve will help you stick to the program of paying yourself first and not going to the well when you don't really need to.

One of the biggest traps to the poverty level life, is that belief that somehow you deserve it. You deserve a new cell phone, a nice car, a tattoo, whatever it is. You don't. You deserve to live and work in a country free from oppression, racism, and the fair and equal opportunity to *earn* the best of the best. Besides, if you earn it you will truly appreciate it. Another trap in a poverty level life is the "need" to be where you are. Sometimes you need to move away from where you are to start somewhere new. Once you have some small level of savings you can leave and go somewhere new. The hardest part is leaving behind the comfort of your previous situation and starting over. Think back to the immigrants who left behind their families and even their entire culture. Traveling thousands of miles with the clothes on their backs to start something new in a country where they might not even speak the language. Don't be tied to your stuff so much that it holds you back. It's just stuff. I know some stuff cannot be replaced, like heirlooms, and those are the more difficult things to part with. However, the place you are isn't the only place in the world. Don't be so stuck on stupid as to not leave an area to explore the possibilities of elsewhere. Especially if elsewhere has more opportunities for you.

I recently heard of someone who owns an Indian restaurant in Wyoming. It is an extremely successful restaurant that people literally travel hundreds of miles to visit. The food sounds so good that the next time I drive across the country, I plan on taking a route that will get me to that restaurant. Perhaps you live in NYC and can make a true NYC style pizza. They don't have many of those in Texas, or Arizona. The cost of living in those states is far cheaper than that of NYC. I know that the fear of the unknown can be truly crippling, and the idea of leaving everything behind to strike out on the open road is not for everyone. I also know that nothing ventured nothing gained. As my momma, Queen says, "Scared money don't win."

Pick your goal. Where is it you want to be? What do you want to have? Now, how will you go forward to earn it? This book is about changing your relationship with money and, in doing so, earn those things you deserve.

Defining your dream and reality

Chapter 3

We all have those dreams of wealth beyond imagination. In all reality, how many Daymond John(s) are there? As an example of bootstrap millionaire, I love this guy. If I could bottle his level of hustle and sell it, we'd all be him. In reality, you can't. However, you can earn your way to a life of comfort and in doing so find your happiness. Yes, it has been said that money can't buy happiness but it sure as hell helps. Here you need to figure out what your dreams are.

When I first joined the Navy, all I wanted was to become debt free, save enough money to buy a sailboat, and become a sailboat bum. No permanent home port. Nothing to tie me down, earn the money I needed for a few beers, a steak occasionally, and maybe Diesel fuel for the engine. I came to this understanding from a time when, as a civilian, I worked for a temp agency. Every morning at 0530 I would get in line with the drunks and the bums living in SoCal and we would wait on tickets to go to work; usually at some construction site picking up trash or moving materials around by hand. It usually paid minimum wage. Many of the guys who worked there lived in tents or under overpasses and all they wanted was enough money to get a pack of smokes, a couple of cheeseburgers, and a bottle of their choice. Usually something cheap and potent. Man, how much I miss those days. No stress if you didn't like the job or the boss, you didn't have to worry about impressing him and sticking around. So long as you weren't a huge F-up you'd have work.

"A sailboat?" I hear you ask. Yes, but I'm not talking about a brand new Beneteau worth $500,000. I'm talking about an older used boat, solid built, not pretty but seaworthy. "But all the expense of a boat?" Yes, and if you live almost anywhere warm enough worth living you can find either open moorage or, as in San Diego, there are mooring balls where you pay almost nothing for the right to tie up your boat, and use a dinghy to get to shore. Think outside the box. Even moorage in a marina will be far less than rent in an apartment in a place like San Diego, CA.

Marriage and children changed this dream. Now it's a beach house hopefully on the Puget Sound of Washington state. Since the dream changed, it is now more expensive. I do have the benefit of a partner to help me live towards this dream. I am very fortunate to have someone who has a similar dream. My dream still includes the bum part. The beach house will be an acceptable compromise to the sailboat. If your lover-partner-spouse isn't onboard with your dream, then are they your lover-partner-spouse? Better said, if your lover-partner-spouse isn't capable of sharing or building a dream with you, are they really that person?

Defining your dream:

What is your dream? Only you can answer this. My dream is not yours. And I'm not here to judge your dream, just help you focus and earn this dream.

The whole and complete point of this book is this:

A goal without a plan, is a just dream.

If this thought doesn't cause the pit of your stomach to drop out, then you just don't get it. And you never will.

Write your dream here:

_____

_____

_____

_____.

Now it is real.

Reality:

Do you know what your dream will cost? Do you have any idea how long it will take to achieve your dream? Is there someone who is going to give you the means to achieve this dream? I didn't think so. What are you going to do about it? That's right go get it!

First thing you need to do is to identify the costs associated with your dream. For me, it's a beach house. Do I want to build or try to find one that fits my dream? I'm choosing to build currently. Why? Because I am still 2 years from retirement and don't want the expense of holding 2 houses at the same time or having to find renters to cover my costs until I can finally go home.

I know I can cover the cost of the land, and when I sell my current house, I will have enough equity to finance the building of the new home. This is a stage or step towards the complete dream. Not all dreams have to be fulfilled in one fell swoop. Many dreams can come in stages.

My first step is to research what it costs to buy land and build a house. The next step is to find the land. Then maybe a builder. Building a house takes up to 10 months. How does this information affect my timeline? There are lots of variables in this dream. You need to spend some time in the fantasy world to plot, plan, and dream about what you really want to understand how to reach that end goal and how much it will cost. Once you have this information you can focus on how to make it happen.

Now it's time to turn your dream into a goal. The younger you are when you can come to the personal understanding of who you are and what it is you want, the easier it will be to achieve it. My mother, God rest her Soul, used to say she didn't want to buy a Mercedes to drive to a job to pay for the Mercedes. She also had champagne tastes on a cheap beer budget. However, it is never too late to understand what you want. Even if you are older, you can make those changes right now. What is that latte worth to you now? As Marie Kondo said, "if it brings you joy…" Does it? Really? Is your lifestyle bringing you joy? I feel the weight of your sigh as you say no. What will bring you joy? You know it, THAT thing right there that makes you smile, your happy place. Now tell the rest to F-off and go to your happy place.

In my heart of hearts, my truly happy place is doing nothing. Nada, zip, F-all. Hanging out with friends, making food, making beer, making love, no work, maybe working on a classic car, or my bike, or definitely a sailboat, maybe building something. When I have enough money to not worry, my happy place is not doing anything I don't want to. Having no bills is my happy place. My debt free life, with no demands on my time is my happy place. There is where I am a FREE man!

So, in your heart of hearts tell me now, what is your happy place?

_____ .

So now you have to strip back the false trappings of success and pursue the true success of your heart. As said by Lao Tzu, "Seek the path of water."

Will designer jeans and shoes help you reach your happy place? Will a big fancy car? What will you give up by not having those things? What will you gain? Are you buying those things because they bring you joy or because you think they will? I love coffee. I own an espresso machine so I can make myself a latte. It's cheaper and tastes better. I love Levi's. All of mine are used and if I didn't tell you, you would never know.

I consider myself the Pied Piper of financial relationship improvement. I want you all to join me on the path. The problem is, I can't tell you what your destination is. I cannot talk to each, and every one of you to guide and mentor you in the right direction. I can only tell you the steps I have taken and why I took them in the directions I did. This worked for me. It can work for you. Even though your dreams are not mine. Your goals are not the same as mine. The endgame is. Best of luck to you. It won't be easy. But it is not impossible. The ultimate reality of it is, if you keep blowing your money on lattes and other stupid things you will never, and I cannot stress this enough, ever have your dream. You must make a choice. Be a wage slave and settle on a mediocre life or define your dreams, create a plan, and make those dreams into goals. Make those goals into reality.

Needs vs. Wants

Chapter 4

We already covered Maslow's hierarchy of needs. To refresh a step, at the bottom of the pyramid are the physiological needs of food, clothing and shelter. Second from the top are the esteem needs or, as I call them, the I-WANT-MEs. Many people confuse the I-WANT-MEs with true needs. This is because the I-WANT-MEs feel so good. A carrot is better for you than chocolate cake but damned if no one ever blows out the candles on birthday carrots.

When my children were very young, I started them on an allowance. They received $4.00 per week. They had to put $1 into their piggy banks, and the rest into their purses. The last Sunday of the month they had to go out and buy what they needed, and then what they wanted. Needs come first.

Right after we started this program, my youngest had started preschool and when I came home from work, she approached me and told me her shoes had broken at school that day. We had just bought them, no big deal, back to the store for an exchange, and good to go. Well, not quite. She had in fact, scraped the toes off her new shoes crawling around on the ground at recess. I made her wear those shoes for the rest of the week and that weekend happened to be what we need and what we want weekend. On Sunday I took her to the store where she had to replace her "broken" shoes. After she got new shoes, I took her to the store and straight to the register where she could buy a couple pieces of penny candy with the little money she had left. Tears were flowing as she realized that she couldn't but a new doll because she had spent her money on what she needed, not what she wanted. Today that young lady, now a teenager, has a bigger wad of loose cash than I do. She learned her lesson that day. Take care of your stuff.

It also only took a few short years on one "What you need and what you want" day, the oldest had a handful of cash to spend on wants and loaded up on the latest little toys. Sitting in the car with her new possessions, all unwrapped ready to enjoy them, she looked up at me as the reality slowly descended upon her. With a mixture of awe and sadness she said, "I don't know why I wanted these. Why did you let me buy them? This was the stupidest thing I have ever done." I looked at her through the rear-view mirror, smiled, and said, "that was the lesson I wanted you to learn." This past Christmas I gave her a used KitchenAid stand mixer; you know the one with all the attachments. I bought it at Goodwill, didn't even wrap it. She LOVED it. I saved about $250, and it was practically brand new, used maybe once.

"May you have all that you need and want all that you have." Anon. I hope these words ring true for you. I know that even for myself there are times when the I-WANT-MEs take over my mind and I NEED something I really don't. I am trying to overcome the need to have something and even now I have a difficult time giving up the things I have but no longer want. I also justify that I already paid for them so why get rid of it. I just might NEED it in the future.

Needs:

What we need in a very simplified context, is food, clothing, and shelter. Anecdotally, it has been said that hunter-gatherer humans spent less time in the pursuit of food, clothing and shelter than agro-industrial humans (us) do. Because their life was spent seeking those things. When the hunter-gatherer is hungry, he hunts, when he is cold, he gets clothing, and when he needs to rest, he builds shelter. When the modern human needs food, he first goes to work to earn money, then goes to the store to buy the food, then to home to cook it, and then finally gets to eat it. Our lives are spent building widgets, earning checks, then spending those checks on food, clothing and shelter. If the modern human is lazy then he goes to work, earns the money, and then goes to the restaurant to buy the food, spending more than double for the same meal.

The same logic applies to clothing and shelter. Although today it is easier, cheaper, and a lot quicker to buy clothing, where modern human gets lost is in the belief that they NEED name brands or to buy only new clothing, or a lot of something. Do you really need 12 pairs of jeans? Probably not. Now, due to sheer numbers of modern populations, we don't live near where we work, we live in such a place that it takes time and money to get to work to earn the checks to pay for the house and transportation. Again, where needs are dominated by wants, we end up spending more money on this aspect of our lives than we need to. I prefer a house in a more suburban location than urban. I want trees and birds, and I don't really mind the occasional trash panda or fox in my yard. To that, I make sacrifices. To me, a car is a means of transportation. I want a safe, reliable vehicle that gets me from point A to point B in relative comfort at a minimal cost. To that end I drive a Toyota Corolla. So does the spouse.

Yes, we also have a 1963 Dodge Dart GT, a motorcycle, and a boat. That said, the Dart was purchased 23 years ago, the boat is from 1967, and the motorcycle is a Yamaha Bolt that I bought used and customized myself. Even so, that doesn't mean that those were responsible purchases. We would have been further ahead had we never spent the money we did for these luxuries. Sometimes you should let the pressure valve out a little, otherwise you will go nuts. You cannot live at the edge forever. You need to reward yourself, just don't go into debt for it. That point we will address soon.

There are many ways to address the needs in your life. We're going to make some assumptions here. This book isn't an attempt to address the serious situations of food deserts in urban locales, nor the plight of astronomical rents that people cannot escape. These are serious and critical flaws in our society, and this isn't the forum to address them. This book is to help people change their relationship with money.

Grocery shopping is possibly one of the worst possible things about adulting. On the other hand, it can be the first, and biggest way to change your relationship with money. Let us start by addressing where you are shopping. I know many people who swear by Trader Joe's, or Wegman's, or Vonn's, or the farmer's market, or any one of the high-end grocery stores because of the vegan, fair trade, organic, overpriced products that they sell. This is no shade thrown on these companies. They have made their market model work, and they deserve it. Just don't expect me to participate here.

I'll start by asking you about that bag of potatoes in your cart. Where were they grown? Oh, those are just regular potatoes? Ok. Did you know that you could have bought those same potatoes at a local discount grocery store for about 1/3 of the price? I see you also have the name brand mac-n-cheese in your cart. Did you know that the bargain basement, store brand, or no name brand is probably made by the same company? Yes, this is 100% true. Think about it, how many companies exist in the world that make mac-n-cheese in a box? Is there that big of a market? I bet there must be some fierce competition in the mac-n-cheese business. Come on, seriously. There are only a few companies out there and they control the entire market. If you don't believe me, go to the websites of Kraft Foods, or Mondelez International, or Nestle, or whomever, and see just how many brands are under their umbrellas. It is staggering. This is no dig on them. This is capitalism at its finest.

My first recommendation is to go to the discount grocery stores, like Aldi's, Lidl, Winco, Sav-u-Foods,

Grocery Outlet, etc., and stock up on the basics. Then go to your frou-frou places for the goodies. You will save thousands of dollars. I do. I love my goodies! How do you think I can afford Goat Cheese bruschetta as a Sunday morning breakfast? Or my custom motorcycle.

Clothing is the next place we spend too much money. You can find name brand clothing, barely worn, in every thrift store in the USA. Today, right now. Yes, in your size. Sometimes it's an adventure in shopping but the rewards are there. Now, I don't buy my basics there. Socks, underwear, etc. No, thank you. I have been known to buy shoes though. Depends on their condition. With the money I save, I am no longer so stretched when it comes to buying the other clothing I need. If you work in a suit and tie environment, you can find some truly classic stuff, for cheap. Take it to the tailor and have it custom fitted and you will still save hundreds of dollars while bragging that you have a custom-tailored suit. The last time I did this, I got a beautiful Yves Saint Lauren blue pinstripe suit and tailoring for $75 total. I looked good too. This is a running joke with my tailor. Yes, I have a tailor. He is the owner of the local dry cleaner and I went to him to have some pants hemmed. In doing so, I realized that he could also take in any suit jacket to fit me. Tada, I have a tailor. Have you ever asked your dry cleaner what they do with their abandoned clothes? Often, they will give you them for the cost of the cleaning. Think about that. A nice fine silk shirt or cocktail dress for less than $10. No joke. You can still get your name brands, just think outside the box. Remember, I told you I bought a Bottega Veneta Jacket for $45 with the tags still on it. It retails for $600. I still don't buy many things at full retail either. No shame here. I will try something on in a store then check out Amazon. Which retailers have gotten wise to, and have come down on their prices. I also wait for the sales. Buying clothing off season is also a great way to save some money. It might not be this season's style, but if you're reading this book, you probably don't care about that. If you do care about that, this book is here to help you get over yourself. Do like I do, stick to the classics of color and style. No one ever said that all any woman ever needs is a little pink bouffant dress. It's a little black cocktail dress. Elegant, simple, classic, sexy. Carrie Bradshaw, am I right?

Housing is one of the biggest needs we have. I am a huge proponent of a safe, comfortable, place to live. This is where needs and wants collide. What we need for housing is very individualistic. I need a place in a good school district. Which means I am going to pay for it. I want a place not too far from work. My commute limit is 30 minutes. Many people think this is too far for them. For me it's just about a perfect motorcycle ride. Time to relax unwind and be ready for the family when I get home. It's also far enough from work that the boss will not be so quick to call me in. I will not confirm if this was intentional. When it comes to buying a house, you make the choices for your lifestyle, needs, and wants. I do suggest that you take into consideration the following. You will die in that house before you sell it again. Seriously. If you buy, thinking this is a starter home, and that in 5 years you will flip it and move into the 'burbs and then get a bigger house, to one day retire and downsize, hopefully to make money when you sell it, you will have lost out in value as you have traded houses around. My advice is to buy the nicest house, one that fits your lifestyle as a function over time, in the best possible neighborhood you can afford, and expect to die in that house. As a function of time is how you look at the rest of your life. Will there be kids? If so, how many? Spouse, dog and cat? Do you need a fenced yard? A yard at all? Then as you examine that function over time, you will come to understand the kind of house that you need. Remember you're going to die there.

The biggest caution I must mention is that if you buy too much house, you could find yourself in a house rich but cash poor situation. Possibly forced to remain in a location, a job or relationship because of what you owe on that house. The myth of the starter house has been one of the biggest vampires to retirement ever. Most people forget that in order to sell your house, you - the seller, will pay the real estate agents involved up to 7% of the sales price. Yes you hope to get it out of the cost of the house, but if you buy a house for $350,000.00 dollars and then sell it for less than purchase price plus 15%, you will lose money because of all of the realtor fees, taxes, costs of your original loan, etc. Each time you buy and sell a house there must have been such inflation to drive your house price up to cover your expenses, which means that the next house will be more expensive too.

If and, when you buy a house, you need to pay it off much faster than the generous 30 years of servitude the bank is offering you. First make sure that your loan doesn't have any penalties for early payoff. Second make sure that any additional money you pay goes to principal and not interest. Some banks make you responsible to notify them that any additional monies paid go to principal. Try not to do business with this type of people they're leeches. They really suck as humans. There are several simple tricks to paying off your house early. The sooner you do, the faster it becomes an asset and not a liability. Remember any debt you have, even the "good debt" of buying a house is a liability. After all, if you owe money to anyone you can never truly be free. If you make 1 extra payment a year you will reduce your mortgage to 26 years instead of 30 to pay it off. Rounding up by approximately $50 per payment could save you another 2 ½ years. By combining those two ideas would shorten your mortgage to under 25 years. This goes up exponentially if you make it an extra $100 a month and two extra payments a year. This is part of the minimum payment mentality that we need to break. I will get into this more soon.

Housing markets are cyclical too. Always better to buy during the off season. Houses for sale at that time are usually cheaper because someone needs to sell. Yes, there is less inventory but remember, take your time and find the right property for you. If you can buy a house that is a little outdated, you can bring it up to more modern tastes relatively cheaply if you're handy with a hammer. YouTube, or your local hardware store, will teach you the rest if you're adventurous and patient.

Modern World, modern needs:

In the US we have a lack of adequate mass transit because we have a love affair with our cars that runs deep in the vein of independence that is the heart of being an American. If you live in the big city where there is a mass transit system, it can get you to work and back in relative comfort and minimal expense.

Therefore, a car becomes a need because reliable transportation is the need. I have seen a married couple in Spain, riding a motorcycle home from the grocery store, she was sitting side-saddle, wearing a skirt, holding the groceries while he slalomed through Barcelona traffic. I don't recommend this, but it did solve their basic need for transportation. For most of us, the car is a symbol of status. It is the second largest purchase we make, and is one usually renewed every six years. If you calculate the average price of a new car at $37,000 and amortize that cost over six years, your monthly expense is $514. See above table. Currently a 2020 Toyota Corolla base model, is $19,600 or $272 per month for six years. The top of the line isn't much more expensive at $22,050 or $306 per month. If you meet your basic needs for a car, you just saved over $250 per month. $3,000 per year, $18,000 over six years. Damn near the price of the next Corolla. I didn't include interest in any of these figures. This changes the numbers, but if your credit is good enough, then 0% interest might be in your future. Which makes it the same as cash but doesn't change the fact that this is still debt. You're just not paying extra for that debt. If you save the difference, then you can pay cash for the next one. Now if you can pay off the car as soon as possible, and keep it longer, you can then bank that extra money you would have paid for the next new car and if you have to step up to a "better" car, it too could be paid in cash.

If you can stretch out the need to buy a new car as long as possible, 10 years or more, you will save two or three times the price of the next car. Eventually you will reach the point where it costs more to keep an older car on the road. Up to that point you can be banking all that extra money into some sort of a growth account. Only tap into it if major repairs or new tires are needed and not incur any debt there either. My Corolla is a 2010 and has 153,000 miles on it. It has been paid for since 2011. It was part of me paying off all of my debt. My wife's 2013 Corolla with 75,000 miles on it, was paid off in 2016 when we sold our house. The people who bought our house paid it off for us. Thank you whoever you are. Don't forget, the same idea of paying extra each month, like the mortgage, will make you pay off that car sooner than later. Again, you have got to kill the mentality of minimum payment as a lifestyle.

Cell phones have replaced the land line as the de facto form of communication as email has replaced the letter. At issue with the cell phone, is the constant need to replace and update the older models. It took almost 100 years to switch to digital transmission of radio and TV, but every few years we grow into a new generation (G) for cell phone communication. Our cell phones don't last despite the astronomical cost. Having to have the latest and greatest cell phone is a waste of money and time. Do you need 3 cameras on your phone? No, not really. You can survive, somehow, I'm sure you'll manage if your phone is a few years older. I currently have a Samsung S7. I think they're on the S20 currently. I don't know. I don't really care. There are several different companies all offering essentially the same level of service. If you buy older, reconditioned phones, you can get a plan that is cheaper than the cost of a good used car.

This is pretty much the same for all aspects of your life. Remember that every $7.25 is one hour of your life. I do understand that some things require purchasing new or the most recent technology, and for those few purchases it is impossible to find a cheaper cost alternative. However, these costs can be offset by making the compromise of limiting the wants to fulfill the actual needs in other areas of your life.

Wants

I like whiskey. On the rocks, yeah, I know typical American, but I like what I like. Wants are those things that are driven by likes. I like fine whiskey. I don't like the price tag. $35 a bottle makes my heart sink, and that isn't even considered very expensive whiskey. So, I searched for a brand that fulfills my likes and my wants and doesn't rape my wallet.

Wants aren't hard to justify. You're an adult. You don't have to justify yourself to anyone except the person in the mirror. And maybe your significant other. Trust me I get it. Oh, how I want that. It would look so good on me. It would make me so happy to have it, I love it, I *need* it. "My Precious. I must have my Precious. Gollum, Gollum." J. R. R. Tolkien. Wants are a fleeting mistress. They don't last because there is always the next want. My wife is good at stopping my wants with one simple question, "how are *You* going to pay for it?" She also knows that if my want-monster is strong enough that it's easiest to give in and let me figure it out. Eventually, one of two things will happen, I'll get it, or I'll drop it. Sometimes now, it takes me weeks to get over it, and sometimes I'll double back to a want later. I don't always get what I want. Not because I can't afford it, but because I have learned to outgrow that want.

The longer that I have pursued this lifestyle, the longer it takes me to decide if my want is worth it. One method I have discovered is to flip a coin. When I sit there with that gnawing feeling of should I buy this, do I really "want it want it" or is this a fleeting mistress, I flip a coin. If heads I buy it, tails I don't. In the moment of reveal, I pay attention to my gut visceral reaction. That reaction will tell me what I really feel. If I feel ambivalent to a yes, then I know I don't really "want it want it". If I feel a pang of loss to a no, then I know it is something I really truly want and then I get it. Sometimes, I wait for 48 hours if it is a yes. Because I got the yes, now let's see if it stands the test of time. If it does then I get it and enjoy it no guilt. I know that the coin toss sounds stupid, but it has helped in more decisions that you'd expect. It doesn't relieve me of responsibility to make dumb decisions, but it tells me my heart. I once used this technique with a young man who was struggling with his desire to go out into the world or pursue a safe and secure life through an internship with a government agency. I spoke to him for an hour about the merits of both, and unable to decide he thanked me for my time. I suggested the coin flip, because I could tell he was trying to convince himself that the safe path was what he wanted. He thought the idea was stupid but agreed. I flipped the coin, and before I turned it over, I said, "Heads you stay here safe and secure, tails you go out and see the world." He agreed. When I uncovered the coin over, he slumped into the chair and the energy shot out of him like I'd knocked him down. "Fuck" he whispered. I told him he had his answer. Two weeks later he walked out the door and never looked back. It was heads, the safe route, and he knew at that moment it wasn't the right decision for him. I never heard from him again, but wherever he is I know he's going to be fine. "You can't always get what you want, but if you try sometimes, you just might find, you get what you need." The Rolling Stones.

Providing for Needs

Chapter 5

This is where you come to understand your economic future as a need. Suze Orman recommends several million dollars in order to be able to retire. That alone is the most daunting thought there is when it comes to retirement. Currently there is a movement known as Financial Independence, Retire Early (FIRE). This movement is based on some of the ideas I have put out here. Knowing yourself and limiting those wants to needs. I believe in a middle of the road approach to both. You need to have enough money to retire. You need to know how much *your* lifestyle is, in order to retire. If you have no base idea how much life costs, then you cannot save enough to be able to retire because you don't know what it is you need. Remember, food, clothing and shelter are your needs.

If average housing costs in the US are $1,500 per month or $18,000 per year, can you find a cheaper place to live? Yes of course. But do you want to live there? Maybe not. Can you change the cost of your housing in your area? Yes. You could share a place with friends, or an alternative living arrangement like a sailboat, an RV, or a mobile home. These ideas aren't a good fit for everyone.

If you work in a place like Seattle, then in order to afford a reasonable place to live you won't be living in Seattle. You will be living in your car on the I-5 just to get to work. BTW, the median home price in Seattle is just shy of a ridiculous $714,000. So, is your self-esteem the reason why you need to live in Seattle? Is it an I-WANT-ME? An esteem need not a physiological need? Probably. Therefore, by living in a different city you will improve your economic situation. It will require the tradeoff of time in your car, and the associated increased costs with more gas, and maintenance. These costs will be much less than the cost of housing in Seattle. These kinds of tradeoffs are at the root of the discussion here. Once you establish a value to them, you can and will begin to make trades in terms of needs and how to satisfy those needs. For example, the Seattle job against the more affordable housing.

If you cannot reduce your expenditures, then you must increase your income. This is not as easy as it sounds. If we all could go out and get more money we would. I can hear you ask how can you provide for your needs when you don't have enough money? How does one go from flat broke to enough to save for tomorrow when today is too expensive? It's no secret. You spend less. Today, tomorrow, and the day after too. Just spend less.

Unconscious spending is the biggest pitfall to an economic plan. I hate the term budget. It is the limit of our language that forces me to use that term. I prefer strategic spending. That you formulate a plan and stick to that plan. A long-term strategy. The unconscious spending is more like tactical spending. Heat of the battlefield as it were. I want a Coke. I bought a Coke. At the gas station, where I paid too much for it. Using a strategic plan, you set yourself up to reduce the possibility of tactical spending. You first divide your expenses into two main categories. Continual expenses, like housing and car insurance. And flexible expenses, like food and gifts.

I recommend watching the TV show, "Till debt do us part." Gail Vaz-Oxlade breaks it down to the simple use of jars and cash. I like her methods and it was some of those same methods I used to get debt free. No single style will work for everyone. I used her method among others to create the method that worked for me. This is what I am sharing with you. My method.

Continual expenses are those that usually don't change over the course of the year. Housing, insurance, sometimes the utilities are continual expenses. These are the expenses you pay in order to provide shelter, and security. Insurance, both car and health, are also those types of expenses. However, you can shop around to find cheaper forms of insurance. In the end when talking car insurance, you need only the most basic of liability if you own your car outright. It may make sense though depending on where you live, to have full coverage, especially if you live in an area with particularly bad drivers. Health insurance, renter's insurance etc. can be opted out of but again, if you choose to do so, the ultimate expense of cash for health care or paying out of pocket for destroying your apartment may drive you to bankruptcy. Continual expenses are bills like the cellphone and internet. Any subscription style account where the monthly cost doesn't change. These bills are not necessarily needs, and you should use extreme scrutiny to determine if these should continue or be eliminated. Here again you can save money by shopping around, picking only the options you really need, and even sharing plans with family and friends. Cellphone companies, streaming services, etc. all have a family plan wherein multiple people can all have their own log in or share the service. If you share this plan with three friends, you each only pay out a percentage of the cost of an individual plan.

Flexible costs are any expenses that tend more towards the want side of expenses. Flexible costs are inconsistent, varying purchase to purchase, month to month. Clothing, gifts, dining out etc. You can choose to give a smaller, more intimate gift to someone vice a big lavish expensive gift. Clothing can be purchased used, or off season. You can choose to eat out at a fast-food place or fine dining. Anything that does not fulfill a physiological need, clothing, shelter or food is a flexible expense. I hear you saying, you said food is a flexible expense. It is. If you buy steak every day, your food budget will be very expensive. If you buy rice and beans, your food budget will be very inexpensive. You have to shop the perimeter of the store, where the real food is. Skip shopping in the premade section of your grocery store, especially skip shopping for name brands. Like I said previously, you can literally save thousands of dollars by buying store brand products from discount grocery stores. Avoid the prepackaged, premade foods that aren't that healthy either and are much more expensive that their whole food counterparts. Organic, fair trade, farm to table, or whatever other boozhy terms for more expensive than necessary are also false traps to avoid. Yes, we all want to buy the best for ourselves, but I promise you fair trade does not include you. And ALL produce is farm to table. Just because they have it at the farmers market doesn't make it fresher than the grocery store. Where do you think the store bought their food from? Remember that it is cheaper at the grocery store because the store bought 10,000 lbs. of it, you're only buying 1 lb. at the market. Like the 20 oz. soda, things are cheaper in bulk for the stores as well.

Transportation costs, like gasoline can be either a continual expense or a flexible expense depending on how you drive. If you only drive to work and to the store, then your gas bill could be a relatively stable expense. If you like to go out for a drive, then your gas bill is a flexible expense. Washing your car vice getting it washed, is another way to reduce car expenses. You may have to keep getting your oil changed by a professional, but you can shop for coupons, go to a discount place like Jiffy Lube or, switch from synthetic oil to regular if your car can support it. You can also reduce your monthly car expenses by ridesharing, using public transit, or walking if you live close enough to work or the grocery store. Here the type of car you drive can greatly affect your monthly expenses. One issue is that many people have cars where they owe more than the cars are worth. This is called being upside down on your car loan or note. With housing we call it being underwater. Here is the dilemma, if you own more than the vehicle is worth, selling it won't alleviate your debt. It won't reduce your operating expenses either and you're stuck with something you cannot afford to drive. A dealership will be happy to take it off your hands and add what you owe onto another car. This may help you reduce your monthly payment and possibly your operating costs. However, it should only be considered if you have no other way of reducing your expenses due to the vehicle and need to free up some cash flow.

Providing for your needs is how we can pare down to the necessary vice the glamorous. Remember what Gordon Ramsey says about food, "Simple, local, elegant." Apply this to your needs and keep them elegant. You won't want for anything.

Providing for Wants

Chapter 6

When you finally know what your needs are, then you can figure out your wants. You need a car. You want a_____. A Cadillac? A Corvette? A Corolla? Maybe you want a 1963 Dodge Dart GT. It really doesn't matter. "But wait you said that you don't need these things." Yes that is correct I did say that. "But wait, now I'm confused." Yes that happens.

Here is where needs and wants can intersect. Perhaps you work construction. You need a work truck, or a cargo van. Maybe you drive long distances, on the road a lot perhaps as a realtor or in some sort of sales. Then you might need a crossover vehicle, something that you can drive clients in comfortably and have the ability to transport items required for your business.

The actual type of vehicle you need does not dictate the cost of that vehicle. I knew a man who was a realtor who tried to justify his fancy new car to me as required for his business. He told me he had to demonstrate a measure of wealth in order to instill confidence in his clients. The reality is he had to justify his wants over his actual needs. A dear friend of mine, who is a wildly successful realtor, hasn't bought a new car in the last 35 years I have known him. Certified pre-owned is his go to vehicle. He won't even buy himself his fantasy car even though he can now afford it because it isn't a practical need. And his fantasy car is now also 35 years old and the best used version available is very reasonably priced. Best of all he can absolutely afford it. But he won't. I wish he would, I'd love to go for a ride in a Porsche. I'd love to see him smile behind the wheel as he achieves a new land speed record, or at least a personal best over the mountains. But it's not his need, and so remains his dream. Good on him for recognizing this.

Tools of the trade can always be justified. Buy it nice or buy it twice. If your livelihood is based in part on having the tools of a professional, then buying a knockoff will be more expensive in the long run. Because you will buy it twice. Again, there are levels of professional requirements. You can always buy tools on sale or from someone who is retiring or leaving the trade. Last year's model will be just as professional as this year's.

When establishing a residence, people tend to go for the fantasy. Matching towels, matching dishes and cutlery. Whatever it is, whatever the fantasy, many people tend to go for the want over the need. Here again, a nice place to live can alleviate a lot of stress, but in affording all the nice can actually compound the stresses of a residence. Nice sheets will last longer than cheap sheets. Now ask yourself, do you really need 1,000 thread count Egyptian cotton? Well, yes, lol of course. Seriously, here buy it nice or buy it twice can go overboard. A residence is one of the largest expenses, and here is one area where wants overdrive needs. It is an easy area to allow your esteem needs to drive your physiological needs because everyone deserves a decent place to live. Discipline here is going to carry you far. Think of your long-term goals. Is this residence part of that plan? If yes, then working towards the fantasy is part of the ability to provide for the want and the need simultaneously. Just don't go into debt to do it. Chip away at it. This month it might be towels. Next purchase may be the sheets. After that, the dishes, and then the cutlery. If you want to make a change in the structure like changing carpet for hardwood floors or vice versa then set that goal and work towards that. Earlier I mentioned that if you're going to buy a house, buy the nicest house you can afford in the best neighborhood you can afford, and expect to die in it. If you buy a fixer upper with the intention to flip it later, then only do the remodel to a neutral level because no one will like all the things you like. Trust me, if you put in granite countertops then the next owner will want butcher block. If you intend on keeping this house, then remodel it to your likes and tastes. Forget what is fashionable and trendy and go with what you like. In the end it won't add value to the house beyond functionality. In the end when you buy a house you are buying a place to eat, sleep, and take care of your hygiene. You can apply this same logic if you rent.

A house is one of the most difficult purchases and sales. People get emotionally attached to their house, and their stuff. No one is going to pay for your feelings. Get over that idea right now. Just because

48

you raised your children in the house doesn't mean I'm not going to paint over their growth chart on the door post within the first few days I move in. As Kevin O'Leary, aka Mr. Wonderful loves to say, "Money doesn't care." You need to be as emotionless as money when it comes to your use of money. Cold and calculated. This is business. *Your* business of paying for *your* life. It should hurt to spend and be a joy to watch as it stacks up. You should never ever be afraid to walk away and keep your money in your pocket.

Wants? What wants. These are my needs. My need to have enough money to not need to worry about working. To fulfill my needs for as long as possible doing as little as possible. To eat well, sleep in a decent bed, enjoy a drink, travel a little, and not worry as I do it.

How about you? When you can focus on your long-term goal, then the little wants are easier to forgo.

Dream come reality

Chapter 7

Let us remind ourselves that a goal without a plan is a dream. You have thought of your dream, now let us make it a reality.

First thing is to decide on your goal. It isn't as easy as it seems if you don't know yourself. My goal is to retire early. The reality of my dream is to retire earlier than most. I hate working with a passion. People say I will get bored, but nope not going to happen. I will always be able to find a way to get in trouble. So, what will it take for me to retire early?

First, I need to secure my physiological needs. Shelter is the number one expense. I want a beach house. Or at least a house with an awesome view. It must have three bedrooms, two bathrooms, and a garage. I'd prefer one story. How much that costs, is going to depend on location. I want to be within one hour of a major city, so that I can get access to food, drink, and some form of entertainment. If you buy empty land, you can have a mobile home dropped for around $100,000. Or a simple stick-built house for around $200,000. You can find cheaper housing or spend as much as you want. For me, it is to build a house under $300,000. Once I retire, I will sell my current house and hope to reinvest approximately $150,000 to get my new mortgage under

$150,000. That should lower my housing costs, including utilities to around $1,000 monthly. I don't want to live in a condo or an apartment. This may be cool with some people, but I'd prefer to not hear my neighbors breathing. All in it looks like $12,000 per year.

The next expense is of course food. Again, this is highly dependent upon location. Food in Hawaii is expensive. Other places not so much. Dining out is also expensive. Using the above data as an average, one can assume that food cost will be at least $500 monthly. This will include eating out but being an adult about it. Annually we're talking about $6,000.

Clothing is one of those expenses that should get cheaper. Not having to work means not having to provide for the work uniform. I don't care where it is you work you have some standard of dress. Even strippers have a uniform. Except for a little black dress, or some similar male equivalent, you won't need to buy a lot of clothes. An easy average for non-working people is probably less than $50 per month. $600 per year per person. Seems like a lot to me.

Health care is one of the expenses that will kill anyone's retirement dreams. According to internet research, the average senior citizen spends $633 per month on health care. This includes the out of pocket expenses of copays, etc. I have skewed that statistic in my favor by retiring from the military. Medicare part B is currently a minimum of $144.60 per person for people who earn up to $87,000 income per year. From the time I retire until I am 65 years old as a military retiree, I will pay $565.20 per year for me and my family through Tricare for Life. By the time I am 65, I will be drawing on my 401k, and Social Security. Although my expenses will increase, my income will also increase enough to cover those costs. Remember that Medicare doesn't cover dental or vision. Eventually my annual costs for health insurance will be approximately $3,500 per year, for me and the spouse. The costs of medical care could have a huge impact on your decision of where to retire. If you retire to somewhere like Mexico, your medical costs could be potentially under $500 per year. In Mexico, you can pay cash for your visit to the doctor, or dentist or eye doctor. Believe me, the care you will receive in Mexico is no less quality than the care you can receive in the USA. When you're talking approximately $20 for a visit to the doctor or dentist, you're going to save potentially 10's of thousands of dollars. You can find the same level of care in many countries around the world.

You can find housing and food costs much cheaper than the US in many wonderful and beautiful places around the world. Don't limit yourself to the US. It could be so much cheaper that you could return to the US multiple times a year and still save more money than living in the US.

If you have been following the math,

Housing	$12,000
Food (per couple?)	$6,000
Clothing (Individual)	$600
Health Care (Couple)	$3,500

==

Total	$22,100

That's right folks just a mere $22k per year for the basics. Add in about $3k just for giggles, like car insurance and who knows what unconscious spending you have, and $25k is it. TWENTY-FIVE THOUSAND DOLLARS PER YEAR! That's a lot of cheddar. It also doesn't include Netflix or Hulu or any of the other myriad of wants we have in life. It is also well below the national average of $64,154 (gross). Remember that you need 90% of your pre-retirement income to maintain lifestyle in retirement. So, $57,738 (gross) or $47,109 take home, from the former table. A senior enlisted person retiring from the military will take home under their legacy retirement system approximately $29,500 annually.

On average $1 million will last 19½ years in America. Then you will be broke. This will be a lot less time in Hawaii (10 years-ish) than in Missouri (22 years-ish). Please note that it will cost approximately $33,000 per year to retire in Missouri. What does that senior enlisted retiree make in retirement? Oh yeah just under $30k.

Now transportation costs are something to argue about. However, on average including the car payment, gas, insurance etc. the average retiree spends approximately $7,000 per year. If you own your car, meaning you have paid off the loan, you could potentially drop this to less than $3,000 annually. Again, back to the discipline thing. If you live in a city with an adequate transit system you could potentially save more, but then your costs convert to increases in housing, food or both. The costs for retirement above do include transportation, wherein my table does not.

If you pare down life to the barest of bones, it could be argued that a couple could retire in relative comfort under $33,000 per year in the United States. With this number you can now begin to massage the dream into a goal.

What will your dream cost?

$_____

Does this include the $33k you will need just to survive? If not, then your dream will cost

$___DREAM___+$33,000.00=_____

If your dream is to replace some of the costs associated with any of the base criteria for survival, like housing, then you will subtract that figure listed above from the cost of your dream plus survival. i.e.

($DREAM+$33,000)-$12,000(HOUSING)=$DREAM+$21,000

You can replace any, or all of the factors for survival with the dream. You cannot eliminate those factors only replace them.

If your plan is to live on a boat, and pay cash for the boat, you will still have additional fees associated with the cost of the boat. Moorage, maintenance, engine fuel, fuel for cooking, etc. These fees can be less than mortgage but may come in around $1,000 per month. As of today, the average price per foot for a slip in Sand Diego, CA. is $15/foot per month or $600 per month for a 40' boat. This does not include electricity, sewage pump out, engine fuel, and fuel for cooking or boat maintenance. Nor does it include storage for your car or toys that don't fit on your boat.

If your plan is to live off the grid in the middle of the forest or desert, and you want to go 100% solar or wind powered, your costs for installation of those things will set you back approximately $30,000 to have enough power to run your house. Heating, cooking, AC, refrigeration. Unless you want to live like a mountain man from the 1800s. You will need to replace solar panels every 20 years on average. Which is $1,500 per year cash output. Which is also the less than my current electricity bill, except you must either pay cash or finance it on credit. The costs associated with building a house in the middle of nowhere also contributes to its final price. Don't forget too, that the associated costs for transportation to get food etc. also increase, as may the costs of food itself. Unless of course you're living like a mountain man from the 1800s.

Is your plan to travel extensively? You may be able to offset your permanent residence costs by using your permanent place as a short-term rental. You will incur costs associated with that through a property management company, who typically charge 10% of rental. You also must have the cash to pay for any maintenance costs or emergent repairs while you're away on your adventures. With any luck you will not be covering the cost of a residence you're not actually using. There are house swapping sites where someone would love to come and stay in your house while you stay in theirs. Think outside the box. Two weeks in Hawaii for two people can set you back up to $7,500 all in. Spain might set you back $4,000. You can of course travel to these places cheaper. It is all a matter of what you're looking for in your vacation. Backpacking around Europe or Hawaii will be much cheaper than staying in hotels. There are many memorable things to do and see that are much cheaper and potentially safer if you use a tour service. You may be locked to their schedule, but every tour service usually has some designated time for the individuals to explore without the set schedule. The average cruise costs $3,000 per person, not including airfare. Again, if this is in your interest, then shop for a deal. Travel off season or sometimes in a bigger group will be cheaper. Be creative too in your choice of destination, and how to get there. You can buy a ticket from NYC to Paris, and then a ticket from Paris to the Seychelles cheaper than flying directly from NYC to the Seychelles. Which by the way, stops in Paris enroute to the Seychelles. With the internet, you can find out about almost everything about your destination, and plan ahead. This will give you the advantage of knowing where to go, how much it might cost, or cultural advice like how much to tip. For example, in some places huge tips are an insult (Italy), and tipping correctly can save you a lot of money, and embarrassment.

Perhaps your dream is to retire somewhere and restore old cars or wooden boats, or antique stained-glass windows, or furniture, make jewelry or blow glass or whatever. Do you need to get an education in how to? You might need to go to school to learn how. If so, is there a school near where you want to retire? If not, how much will that cost you? If you want to attend the Northwest School of Wooden Boat Building, all in for one year, tuition, fees, and housing is $41,000. If Port Hadlock, Washington is not where you want to retire then you will have to add that factor to the costs of your dream. Then, once you move you will incur the costs of property for a boat yard, preferably by the water so you can put your boat back into the water or, pay rental fees to someone who has a boat yard usually $2/foot per day, increasing every 2 weeks. Don't forget the other associated fees like hauling your boat in and out of the water, stepping and un-stepping the mast, crane service. All these fees are part of that dream. If it is cars you want to restore, do you have a place with a garage big enough to do real mechanics work in? Do you need a lift, compressor, or paint room? Remember the older the car the more the parts become expensive and harder to find. Each dream has costs that are extra to the basics of survival, and you need to be conscious of those costs. These are the costs of retirement. Unless all you want to do is sit around and stare at the walls. Which is totally fine. I just don't know many people that would satisfy.

Perhaps reading books and puttering around in a small garden are your goal. This is probably the cheapest goal you can obtain. On average in the US, people spend $400 per year gardening. Also, the local library is free. Minus the cost of transportation to the library. Which if you're crafty you link your trips to the library with your trips to the grocery store and then your added costs are minimal. There are plenty of other small hobbies you can add to this kind of lifestyle that are relatively low-cost barrier to entry. Meaning that they are cheap to start and maintain. For me, I love the art of building ship in a bottle models.   I have only done one in my life so far, mostly due to time availability.   The cost of the tools and materials are very cheap.   An empty bottle, some scraps of wood, and a few sharp Xacto style blades are almost all that you need to create something beautiful.

Whatever your goal ultimately is, will depend on what you want.   Yes, your retirement goal is a want. Very few people around the world ever live long enough to retire.   The global average life expectancy is 72.6 years.   Many developed countries have retirement ages above 62.   The actual number of people who do retire is far less than those who work until they die.   Currently only half of all working Americans actually retire by 65.   Remember the average American life expectancy is 79.   So how will you cover your costs for 14 years? Social security? That won't cover half of your expenses. Most Americans have only $17,000 in savings by the time they are ready to retire.   69% of Americans no longer work full time by 65 years old, and only 51% of all Americans stop working altogether.   By age 75, almost 90% of all Americans stop working, but they're dead four years later anyway.

In returning to the idea of making your dream a reality.   What are you going to give up, to reach that goal?   What is your timeline?   When will you have to begin saving in order to reach that goal?

Working Backwards

Chapter 8

Once you have a price tag on your goal, you can now establish benchmarks or milestones to that goal. If you need to have $1 million in cash by 60 years of age, how much cash should you have by 50? By 40? 30? Well that depends on where your starting line is.

My starting line was in 2010. I was 40½ years old. I had been in the military for 8 years and knew I was going to do 20. I knew I would have a approximately $25,000 per year in passive income after I was eligible to retire. If I could retire at 52½ years old, and hopefully survive to 79 then I would receive approximately $662,500. I knew that at 59½ I could begin to draw on my 401k, known as the TSP in the military, and if I invested correctly, I should be able to draw another $12,000 per year. Or $240,000 total. That means that I had managed to save almost $902,500. At 62½ I will draw on social security and the average for a couple will be $2,448 monthly, or $29,376 annually. So, if I continue to work until I can draw my social security, I know I will be able to draw approximately $66,376 annually, all sources combined. Which is close to the median income for retirees. The above figures while seeming like hard numbers were/are really written in water. I was guessing at the amount I would receive in retirement as my pension. It is actually higher. The amount of money I will be able to draw from my 401k is higher too. And every so often the government does something nice like raise the annual social security payments. Ultimately, you cannot know what these figures will be until you are in a closer proximity to retiring. Usually less than five years from the magic date you will be better able to pinpoint your costs and income. It is also at this time that you should begin to fully shift your focus towards the retirement lifestyle.

That was my goal. But my goal post is shorter than most. I plan on retiring at 52½. When I retire from the Navy I want to retire completely. Don't tell me that I'll get bored, blah blah blah. You don't know me. Maybe I like being bored. This is my goal. Whatever your goal is, is just that, *Your* goal. This is mine. Therefore, I need to have some means to make enough money to cover the gap between 52½ when I retire and 59½ when I start to draw on my 401k. Which is $41,376 annually. $289,632 total. And from that gap to 62½ when I will begin to draw on social security. $29,376 annually. $146,880 total. For a combined total of $436,512. Or is it possible that my expenses will be that huge difference. And when I start to draw my money from 401k and/or social security I will have more money that I need? Yes, that is the plan. Mostly. Once your goal is defined, your spending habits must come into alignment with your ultimate goal. If you have a goal but don't work for it, you still only have a dream. "Time to get busy living or get busy dying." Andy Dufresne, Shawshank Redemption.

By establishing milestones, you can measure your rate of success in obtaining your goal. Begin with the simple step of defining your objective. Once your objective is defined, define the costs associated with obtaining your goal, and the steps to reach those costs. If you know you need $1 million, and you currently earn $50,000 how many years will it take you to reach that goal? Twenty years if you could save every penny. Since that isn't possible, how do you earn more money? Can you move your goal post? Is there some element you're not factoring in to the million-dollar equation? Like social security as a portion of that million? Other factors to obtaining that goal are reducing monthly expenses. Could you live in a single wide trailer? I did, during the 14 months it took me to pay off my debts. Maybe share an apartment with someone and thereby reduce housing costs. Whatever factors you change represent a small victory in the final goal. Each small victory matters. They teach the Navy SEALS, that just one more step can be a victory. Every task is comprised of smaller elements and the successful completion of each small task results in successful completion of the objective. If your objective has 15 minor steps, you then have 15 smaller victories that result in the domination of your objective. Using this technique in your plan, you establish numerous opportunities to gauge your successes. As you approach each milestone, you are given the opportunity to refocus or redirect your efforts if you see that your current approach isn't as successful as you had hoped for.

It is critical to be flexible in your approach. To be too dogmatic will result in your inability to find a solution that could be a better fit or reduce a previously held obstacle to your success. During the writing of this book, I came to realize that I could find a property with an amazing view just up from the beach for 40-50% less than the property on the beach. That savings will translate into a huge reduction in my costs of housing which helps reduce my overall need for additional money during the gap from 52 ½ to 62 ½ years of age. I will have to give careful thought to see if this is somewhere, I can compromise. If I can, then I could potentially save 30% on my housing costs overall. If not, then I need to find another area where I will compromise. A plan well thought out, with measurable benchmarks will help me stick to the plan and focus my efforts where they will be more successful.

Find some way to chart out your plan. It needs to be written down, made concrete. If it is all in your head, it remains in the fantasy world. It remains a dream.

Final Thoughts

Chapter 9

This is a lifestyle change. You cannot keep spending your money like it is limitless and expect to have anything more than memories later in life. Memories are great but economic stress will ruin your life. You only deserve what you earn. No one owes you anything. Your rights are life, liberty and the pursuit of happiness. You are not guaranteed to achieve it. Stop acting like it's owed to you.

Define your dream. Then create a plan to obtain it. Change that dream into a goal. Fight on until you achieve it. Revel in your success. Teach someone else how you did it. Spread the love. Don't fall victim to the idea that you can keep up with the Jones's. Be your own Jones. You will be happier, healthier.

Remember this.

Afterword:

Here is my reading list. In the order that I believe should be the most beneficial. My thanks to all the authors for their knowledge and commitment to share, what have been life changing ideas and philosophies.

The Richest Man in Babylon by George S. Clason.
Who Moved My Cheese by Spencer Johnson, MD.
Rich Dad, Poor Dad by Robert T. Kiyosaki.
The Courage to be Rich by Suze Orman.
The Nine Steps to Financial Freedom by Suze Orman.
Your Money or Your Life by Joe Dominguez and Vicki Robin.
The Automatic Millionaire by David Bach.
Mad Money by Jim Kramer.

And of course, the TV show you need to binge watch, "Till debt do us part." Hosted by Gail Vaz-Oxlade.

Acknowledgments:

Here is my moment to go Hollywood and thank everyone who has helped me get here. If I fail to mention you directly, please know that you are a huge part of my success as a person. Your influence has given me the tools and abilities that govern my life today.

First to my oldest and dearest friend, Trey. You were the one who first put a finance book in my hand. The fantasy of how we would stack up our money and the commitment that the first one to make a million dollars first has to hire the other as his butler. Only now we know how little $1 million is.

Second, Mike, for your influence to look towards the outside of the box for a broader scope meaning. It was a fateful day, when you knocked on my door with that chunk of lumber.

David and Erin. Friends who remind me that a huge part of life is the fantasy. But like a good friendship, it requires action. Thanks again Erin for editing this mess.

Nate, who showed me how to front load at work so that it was possible to play later. This is fundamental to the lessons I have tried to teach here.

Ms. Tamica B. at the Fleet and Family Service Center, FT. Meade, thank you for the training on how to teach these simple yet profound skills to the dozens of financial mentors and the thousands of service members whom you have helped with their money.

My parents for the foundation that they laid, life's lessons, and skills for how an adult should walk in the world. My Momma-Queen for your oft heard phrases, "You have got to take care of yourself first," and "No man is going to provide for me and mine, I've got to provide for myself" and of course "Scared money don't win." These are what I am talking about here.

Finally, my wife, without whom I would have only settled for only being a bum.

About the author:

Richard Mullen was born a Navy brat, in North Kingstown, RI, his family eventually settled in Tacoma, WA. After graduating from Henry Foss High School in Tacoma in 1987, he attended Pacific Lutheran University. He graduated Magna Cum Lucky with a degree in Political Science in 1991. After a varied career including restaurants, construction, teaching, and lots of failure, he enlisted in the Navy in 2002. During his tenure in the Navy, Richard obtained his MBA, Summa Cum Laude, from Trident University International. Through the United States Military Apprenticeship program, Richard was certified as Counselor, career and kindred. Eventually he became a Command Financial Specialist, a financial mentor to junior and senior Sailors. Richard has deployed four times, earned five Navy Achievement medals, one Joint Service Achievement medal, one less Good Conduct medal than he should have, as well as several unit awards. He presently continues on active duty, with less than 2 years until he retires.

www.ingramcontent.com/pod-product-compliance
Lightning Source LLC
Chambersburg PA
CBHW021502210526
45463CB00002B/846